Sanjeev Kapoor's

Tasty Eating
for Healthy Living

In association with Alyona Kapoor

- Volume Four -

PopulaR
prakashan

www.popularprakashan.com

Published by:

POPULAR PRAKASHAN PVT. LTD.

301, Mahalaxmi Chambers

22, Bhulabhai Desai Road

Mumbai 400 026

for **KHANA KHAZANA PUBLICATIONS PVT. LTD.**

© 2010 **Sanjeev Kapoor**

First Published 2010

First Reprint 2010

(4305)

ISBN – 978-81-7991-557-8

Nutritionist: Kirti Masurkar

Book Design: Pratibha Gurnani Creative

Photography: Bharat Bhirangi, Alim Bolar

Food Stylist: Anupa Das

Printed in India

Standard Press (India) Pvt. Ltd.,

34G, Poothayammal Nagar,

Near YRTV School, Sivakasi - 626 123.

contents

Food Myths   4

Food Substitutes   6

Reducing Salt & Sugar   8

Cereals & Breads

Makai Palak Pulao   12

Lotus Root and Leaf Rice   15

Jammu ka Aloo Anaardana Parantha   16

Brown Rice Vegetable Pilaf   17

Paneer Kulcha   18

Panchranga Pulao   19

Green Fried Rice   20

Jodhpuri Vegetable Pulao   21

Qabooli   22

Tex Mex Pasta   24

Healthy Protein Pulao   26

Cauliflower and Lemon Rice   27

Handi Biryani   28

Clay Pot Rice   30

Erra Saadam   32

Seafood Pad Thai   34

Methods of Cooking   36

Dals & Kadhis

Vrat ki Kadhi   42

Aamras ki Kadhi   43

Methiwali Arhar Dal   44

Khatti Meethi Dal   46

Banjari Dal   49

Gujarati Kadhi   50

Punjabi Kadhi   51

Punjabi Rajma   53

Sambhar   54

Sindhi Kadhi   56

Dal Chenchki   57

Tomato Rasam   58

Leeli Tuvar ni Kadhi   60

Dal Lucknowi   61

Pickles & Chutneys

Gor Keri   65

Teekha Nimbu Achaar   66

Tamatar ki Chutney   67

Red Chilli-Garlic Chutney   68

Sarson ki Chutney   69

Kairi ki Launjee   70

Green Chutney   72

food myths

Food is associated with many myths that sometimes have no scientific basis. You have to decide what is right or wrong for you. The fundamental principle is never to follow anything blindly.

O Grandma says welcome the child with honey: In earlier times, people were not aware that the newborn baby should be given only mother's milk. Only that is perfect for digestion and has no risk of infections. Honey (or jaggery water) can contain bacteria, which can make the baby sick.

O Papaya is harmful for pregnant ladies: Papaya is rich in Vitamin A the need for which increases during pregnancy. Unripe papaya might create problems, but ripe papaya can be eaten.

O Children catch a cold if they eat sour fruits: All sour fruits have abundant vitamins, especially Vitamin C which is excellent for increasing immunity. In fact, studies show that children who eat citrus fruits are not prone to cough and cold.

O Starving is the best way to lose weight: Starving makes the metabolism sluggish and thereby one cannot burn the excess calories, and until that happens one can never lose weight. Eat frequent small meals if you plan to lose weight. The selection of foods is very important.

O Fat-free means calorie-free: Certainly not. 'Fat-free' means free of trans-fat (bad fat) but there are calories present.

O Onion-milk combination or fish-cream combination in a recipe causes skin pigmentation: Not true. There is no scientific backing for this claim.

O Microwave is good only for re-heating: In reality, apart from cooking all types of vegetarian and non-vegetarian foods, a microwave oven is also extremely useful for defrosting, boiling, baking etc.

O Microwave ovens emit radiation that is harmful to health, so much so that it could cause cancer: Truth is microwave ovens are non-ionising appliances; they do not change the physical and chemical properties of food. Microwaves are just another form of energy and are totally safe.

O You cannot deep-fry in olive oil because olive oil has a lower smoking point than other oils: Not true. Olive oil's smoking point is about 375°F and most frying is done below that.

O Boiling water destroys pathogenic micro-organisms: Not true. Boiling does not destroy even micro-organisms, let alone heavy metals, pesticides, herbicides, nitrates, phenol or oil products. So, this is not enough for its purification. Besides, beneficial salts of calcium and magnesium settle at the bottom of the pan after boiling.

O Liver is very nutritious: Not completely true. The liver certainly stores many vitamins, minerals and protein, but it also contains a lot of fat and bad cholesterol, which can be harmful.

O Searing meat seals in the juices: Not true. Experiments showed that when identical pieces of meat were cooked with and without searing both of them lost same amount of weight during the cooking process. While searing certain chemical reactions take place creating new flavours which enhance the dish.

O Use water instead of milk when making scrambled eggs and omelettes because milk makes eggs tough: In reality not only does milk make them softer but also adds more flavour.

O One always gains weight when one stops smoking: Not true. Well, some people also lose weight or stay the same! Weight gain, if there is any, is always short-term weight gain. It is far healthier to be an overweight non-smoker than to continue smoking for fear of putting on weight.

O Low-fat milk has less calcium than full-fat milk: Actually the reverse is true. Skimmed milk and semi-skimmed milk have more calcium because the calcium is in the watery part, not the creamy part.

O Bananas are fattening: Bananas are actually low in fat. There is only half a gram of fat and 95 calories in a banana. They are terrific, hygienic and handy as a snack.

O Most of the heat in chillies lies in the seeds: Not true. Most of the capsaicin, (the compound that gives chillies their spiciness), is contained in the white flesh to which the seeds cling. The seeds have little or no capsaicin but taste hot because when you cut a chilli open, capsaicin is released and absorbed by the seeds. Therefore by removing the seeds the spiciness is not lessened.

O All thickening agents function in the same way: Not true. Different thickening agents like wheat flour, refined flour, cornflour and arrowroot function differently and add different flavours too.

O A potato can save a salty soup or stew: Not true. If you remove the raw potato from the soup, the potato will taste salty as it has simply soaked up some of the salty liquid. Still, there is hope for salty stews: adding a bit of vinegar or sugar can cancel out the saltiness by giving your taste-buds competing flavours.

O Baking soda and baking powder last forever: True and false. Baking soda will still have power a decade on, but baking powder has a shelf life of about a year. What's the difference? Both are leavening agents, but baking powder contains an acid that allows it to react in recipes as soon as it gets wet, giving off the carbon dioxide that makes a cake rise. Baking soda has no acid; it relies on acids in the batter to activate it. If baking powder gets wet or is stored in a humid environment, its potency is diminished. To find out if your baking powder is still good, put some in a glass of water. If it bubbles, use it.

make some healthier choices

Instead of	Eat
Aloo parantha	Gobhi/mixed vegetable parantha, dry-roasted
Biryani, pulao, khichdi	Brown rice biryani, soya-brown rice biryani and brown rice khichdi
Butter chicken	Grilled chicken tikka or tandoori chicken
Caesar salad/Waldorf salad	Mixed green salad with dressing on the side
Cashew nut paste	Melon seed paste
Cheesecake	Low-fat ice cream topped with fresh fruit
Coconut gravies	Onion-tomato gravies
Cream cakes	Oatmeal and bran muffins, date-and-walnut cake
Cream of chicken soup	Clear chicken soup with vegetables
Egg bhurji	Egg bhurji made with extra vegetables
Foods labelled "enriched"	Foods labelled "fortified"
French fries	Baked potato
Fried papad	Papad cooked in the microwave or roasted on gas flame
Fried samosa	Samosa baked in the oven
Fried stuffed bhindi	Stuffed bhindi cooked with very little oil
Fruit juices, milk shakes	Whole fruits, fruit salad without sugar, skimmed milk milkshakes
Groundnuts, dried fruits	Flax seeds, almonds, walnuts in moderation
High-fat milk	Low-fat skimmed milk
Ice cream sundae with sauces	Low-fat ice cream with chocolate sprinklers
Kadai vegetables	Tawa vegetables
Kulfi	Home-made shrikhand made with low-fat yogurt

Instead of	Eat
Maida roti, white bread, pasta	Wheat or jowar, bajra or mixed-flour roti, wholewheat or multi-grain bread, wheat pasta
Mayonnaise	Drained hung yogurt with mustard and a pinch of sugar
Medu wada	Steamed idli
Microwaved caramel popcorn	Air-popped salted popcorn
Mutton keema	Keema of chicken breast
Noodles	Rice noodles or vermicelli
Pakora/bhajia	Handvo/dhokla
Pesto sauce	Tomato pasta sauce
Processed cereals and biscuits	Oats, muesli, wheat bran, wheat germ
Processed oil	Olive oil, canola oil, wheat germ oil, rice bran oil, soya bean oil, mustard oil, small servings of ghee (cow's milk)
Rasmalai	Kheer made with skimmed milk
Red meat	Lean cuts
Rice kheer	Brown rice kheer
Shell fish, crabs	Salmon, mackerel, hilsa, tuna
Sour cream	Buttermilk
Sugar	Artificial sweeteners, jaggery, honey
Tartare sauce	Tomato ketchup
Thepla	Dry-roasted thepla made with no oil or ghee
Thick and rich gravies	Bean sprouts, raw vegetables
Vanilla ice cream	Fruit juice bar
White rice	Brown rice
Yogurt, paneer, cheese	Skimmed milk yogurt, skimmed milk flavoured yogurt, low-fat paneer (skimmed milk or cow's milk), low-fat cheese

how do I reduce salt in my diet?

Approximately 40% sodium by weight, salt is a combination of sodium and chloride. The truth is, our bodies need sodium to help us regulate blood pressure and blood volume. Sodium also assists in keeping our muscles and nerves in tiptop shape. But as in all things, moderation is the ultimate key.

Here are some tips that can help you reduce salt in the daily diet:

❶ Choose fresh fruit, unsalted nuts or plain popcorn over *chiwda, ganthia, sev, chakli,* salted nuts and savoury biscuits.

❷ Avoid processed and convenience foods since these are often loaded with salt.

❸ Try not to add salt to food at the table. Try adding pepper or other ground spices.

❹ Choose products that have reduced salt content, such as unsalted butter.

how do I reduce sugar in my diet?

Sugar is the richest source of carbohydrates, also known as "empty calories". It is advisable to have as little sugar as possible, as excess sugar or carbohydrates are converted to fat and deposited in the fatty tissue of the body. Sugar is metabolized only by all the accessory nutrients like vitamins and minerals. Under the circumstances, the continued consumption of refined sugar can result in the body becoming increasingly deficient in important nutrients.

❶ Use dried fruits or dried fruit purées to replace sugar, particularly in desserts.

❷ Add fresh fruits as natural sweeteners. Fruit sugar does not allow the blood sugar levels to fluctuate.

❸ Cut out sugar in hot beverages. Have mineral water or unsweetened fruit juices rather than sweet fizzy drinks.

❹ If you get sugar or sweet cravings go for natural sweet fruits or substitute the sugar with jaggery but avoid sugar-coated sweets, pastries and biscuits.

❺ Limit the intake of mithai – *barfi, jalebi, laddoo, peda* or *gulab jamun.* Reserve them for special occasions.

❻ Limit the use of sugar/jaggery (*gur*) in cooking.

❼ Avoid condensed milk.

ereals & breads

makai palak pulao

Ingredients

¾ cup corn kernels, blanched
2 medium bunches (700 grams) fresh spinach, chopped
1¼ cups Basmati rice
1½ teaspoons oil
1 teaspoon cumin seeds
1 bay leaf
2 cloves
5 black peppercorns
2 green cardamoms
2 black cardamoms
1 inch cinnamon
1 blade mace
1 inch ginger, chopped
4-6 garlic cloves, chopped
2-3 green chillies, slit
Salt to taste
1 tablespoon lemon juice
1 teaspoon *garam masala* powder

Method

❶ Soak the rice in three cups of water for half an hour. Drain and cook in four cups of water till three-fourth done. Drain.

❷ Heat the oil in a non-stick *kadai*. Add the cumin seeds and when they begin to change colour, add the bay leaf, cloves, peppercorns, green and black cardamoms, cinnamon and mace. Stir-fry for ten seconds.

❸ Add the ginger, garlic and green chillies. Cook over medium heat for one minute.

❹ Add the corn and continue cooking for two or three minutes. Add the spinach and rice and cook, stirring gently for about a minute.

❺ Add the salt, lemon juice and *garam masala* powder and stir. Lower the heat, cover the pan and continue cooking for about five to seven minutes, or till the rice is completely cooked.

❻ Serve hot.

Spinach or *palak* is a rich source of beta-carotene. Its function is to improve the eyesight and protect the heart and skin. It is also rich in folic acid and thereby improves the levels of blood haemoglobin.

lotus root and leaf rice

Ingredients

2 lotus roots
4 lotus leaves
1½ cups rice, soaked
3-4 oyster mushrooms
1 medium green capsicum, seeded and cut into ¾-inch pieces
1 medium red capsicum, seeded and cut into ¾-inch pieces
1 medium yellow capsicum, seeded and cut into ¾-inch pieces
1 inch ginger, grated
2 tablespoons soy sauce
½ teaspoon black pepper powder
Salt to taste
1 teaspoon sugar
2 teaspoons rice wine
¼ teaspoon MSG (optional)

Method

❶ Peel and wash the lotus roots thoroughly under running water and slice thinly. Parboil in two cups of salted water. Drain.

❷ Soak the oyster mushrooms in one cup of hot water for five minutes. Drain and slice.

❸ Wash and wipe the lotus leaves dry.

❹ Drain and boil the rice in four cups of water till three-fourth done. Drain thoroughly.

❺ Mix together the rice, lotus roots, mushrooms, capsicums, ginger, soy sauce, pepper powder, salt, sugar, rice wine and MSG. Divide the mixture into four equal portions.

❻ Spread the leaves on a flat worktop, place one portion of the rice mixture in the centre of each leaf and fold up the edges neatly. Secure with a string.

❼ Heat sufficient water in a steamer, place the rice parcels in it and steam for fifteen to twenty minutes.

❽ Open the parcels and serve hot.

Open the steamer and the aroma completely envelops you. You could well become a dimsum chef! Lotus root is low in saturated fat and cholesterol. It is high in dietary fibre, potassium and Vitamin B, making it a favourite vegetable in weight-loss diet plans.

jammu ka aloo anaardana parantha

Ingredients

2 large potatoes, boiled and mashed
1 teaspoon dried pomegranate seeds, roasted and powdered
2 cups wholewheat flour
Salt to taste
2 tablespoons skimmed milk
2 tablespoons skimmed milk yogurt
1 small onion, chopped
½ teaspoon red chilli powder
2 green chillies, chopped
1 teaspoon *chaat masala*
2 tablespoons chopped fresh coriander

Method

❶ Place the wholewheat flour in a bowl and add salt, milk, yogurt and sufficient water and knead into a soft dough. Cover with a damp cloth and set aside for fifteen minutes. Divide the dough into eight portions.

❷ Add the onion to the mashed potatoes along with the salt, chilli powder, green chillies, roasted dried pomegranate seed powder, *chaat masala*, fresh coriander and salt and mix well. Divide into eight portions.

❸ Roll out each portion of the dough into a small *puri*, place one portion of potato filling in the centre, gather the edges together and roll out into a ball. Further roll into a *parantha*.

❹ Heat a *tawa*. Place one *parantha* at a time on the *tawa* and roast for half a minute. Flip and moisten the *parantha* with a little water. Flip again and moisten the other side too.

❺ Continue to roast till both the sides are evenly browned.
❻ Serve hot.

Aloo parantha with a dieter's touch! Do brush with butter for the kids... *parantha* as a whole is an energy-giving food. Wholewheat flour contributes more dietary fibre than refined flour.

brown rice vegetable pilaf

Ingredients

1½ cups brown rice
2 medium carrots, cut into ½-inch cubes
10-12 French beans, cut into ½-inch pieces
¼ medium cauliflower, separated into small florets
6-7 medium fresh button mushrooms, halved (optional)
½ cup green peas, shelled and blanched
1 bay leaf
2-3 cloves
1 teaspoon cumin seeds
1 inch cinnamon
Salt to taste
2 green chillies, slit
2 tablespoons chopped fresh coriander

Method

❶ Soak the brown rice in four to five cups of water for two hours. Drain and set aside.

❷ Heat a deep non-stick pan, add the bay leaf, cloves, cumin seeds and cinnamon and roast for a few seconds or till fragrant. Add the drained rice and salt and roast for one to two minutes. Add four cups of water. Bring it to a boil.

❸ Add the carrots, French beans, cauliflower, mushrooms and green chillies. Stir and bring to a boil. Reduce heat, cover and cook till almost done.

❹ Add the green peas and mix gently. Cover and cook till done.

❺ Serve hot, garnished with the fresh coriander.

Note: It becomes a little sticky.

If the need is for a one-dish balanced meal, then this pilaf is a winner. Brown rice with vegetables is abundant in vitamins and minerals and the aroma of the spices whets the appetite.

paneer kulcha

Ingredients

Kulcha dough
1 cup refined flour
1 cup wholewheat flour
½ teaspoon baking powder
¼ teaspoon soda bicarbonate
½ teaspoon salt
1 teaspoon sugar
½ cup skimmed milk
1 tablespoon skimmed milk yogurt
1 tablespoon rice bran oil

Filling
200 grams skimmed milk cottage cheese,
grated
2 green chillies, chopped
2 tablespoons chopped fresh coriander
Salt to taste

Method

❶ Sift together the refined flour and wholewheat flour with baking powder, soda bicarbonate and salt into a bowl. Add the sugar, milk, yogurt and one-fourth cup of water. Knead well into a medium-soft dough.

❷ Apply the oil on the dough, cover with a damp cloth and set aside for one hour.

❸ Divide the dough into four equal portions and shape into balls.

❹ Place the cottage cheese in a bowl. Add the green chillies, fresh coriander and salt and mix well. Divide into four equal portions.

❺ Preheat an oven to 180°C/350°F/Gas Mark 4.

❻ Place the dough balls on a lightly-floured worktop. Flatten them slightly. Place a portion of the cottage cheese filling in the centre of each, gather the edges and seal. Cover with a damp cloth and rest for five minutes.

❼ Flatten each ball between your palms and make a nine-inch-round disc.

❽ Place the *kulchas* on a baking tray and bake in the preheated oven for about fifteen minutes. You can also cook the *kulchas* on a *tawa* till both the sides are evenly cooked.

❾ Alternatively you can place the *kulcha* on a cushioned pad and stick onto the inside walls of a moderately hot *tandoor* and bake for three to four minutes.

❿ Serve hot.

Soft *kulcha* with cottage cheese stuffing. Good enough to eat on its own! It is wholesome and keeps the energy levels high in children, so is a great choice for packed lunch.

panchranga pulao

Ingredients

2 medium onions, sliced
1 medium carrot, diced
6-8 French beans,
cut into 1-inch pieces
½ medium cauliflower,
separated into small florets
¼ cup shelled green peas
1 medium green capsicum,
cut into 1-inch pieces
1½ cups Basmati rice, soaked
1 tablespoon ghee
1 inch cinnamon
3-4 green cardamoms
3-4 cloves
7-8 black peppercorns
2 bay leaves
1 teaspoon cumin seeds
Salt to taste

Method

❶ Heat the ghee in a non-stick deep pan; add the cinnamon, cardamoms, cloves, peppercorns, bay leaves and cumin seeds and sauté till fragrant.

❷ Add the onions and sauté till translucent. Add the carrot, French beans, cauliflower and green peas and cook for one minute.

❸ Add the soaked rice and stir-fry for one minute. Stir in four cups of water and salt to taste. Bring to a boil and cook over medium heat for three or four minutes, or until all the water has been absorbed (stirring occasionally).

❹ Stir in the capsicum, lower the heat and cook, covered, for six to eight minutes, or till the rice and vegetables are cooked.

❺ Remove from heat and leave to stand for five minutes. Serve hot.

I personally think this is a wonderful recipe to make vegetables more alluring for fussy children and adults!

green fried rice

Ingredients

10 fresh spinach leaves, chopped
8-10 small broccoli florets, blanched
5-6 French beans, cut into diamonds and blanched
1 medium green capsicum, seeded and cut into diamonds
2 spring onion greens, chopped
3 tablespoons green chilli sauce
1½ cups rice, boiled
1 tablespoon olive oil
2 medium onions, sliced
Salt to taste
½ cup bean sprouts

Method

❶ Heat the oil in a non-stick pan. Add the onions and sauté.

❷ Add the broccoli, French beans and green chilli sauce. Stir and add the capsicum and salt. Sauté for a minute and add the bean sprouts and spinach. Adjust the salt and sauté for one more minute.

❸ Add the rice and mix well and cook till heated through.

❹ Add the spring onion greens and mix again.

❺ Serve hot.

A different dish indeed! Especially for those who can be fussy about their greens, broccoli is rich in Vitamins B, C and A.

jodhpuri vegetable pulao

Ingredients

12 small florets of cauliflower
¼ cup fresh green peas
15 cashew nuts, halved
10 almonds, halved
4-5 dried dates, chopped
1 tablespoon raisins
1½ cups Basmati rice, soaked
1½ tablespoons ghee
1 teaspoon cumin seeds
½ teaspoon fennel seeds
1 tablespoon ginger paste
1 tablespoon garlic paste
Salt to taste
¾ cup skimmed milk yogurt
½ teaspoon *garam masala* powder
10-12 black peppercorns, crushed

Method

❶ Heat one tablespoon ghee in a deep non-stick pan. Add the cumin seeds and fennel seeds and sauté till fragrant. Add the cashew nuts, almonds and dried dates and sauté for a minute.

❷ Add the cauliflower florets, ginger paste, garlic paste, raisins and salt and sauté for another minute.

❸ Add the rice and yogurt and mix. Add two cups of water and *garam masala* powder and mix well. Bring to a boil, reduce heat, cover and cook till half done.

❹ Add the green peas and stir. Cover and cook on medium heat till done.

❺ Sprinkle the crushed peppercorns and remaining ghee. Stir gently and serve hot.

This *pulao* has a touch of royal Rajput cooking as there are various nuts and dried fruits added to it. The cauliflower adds potassium and the green peas, Vitamin C. Fennel adds freshness and aids digestion.

qabooli

Ingredients

1¼ cups rice
½ cup split Bengal gram
Salt to taste
4-5 green cardamoms
2 one-inch cinnamon sticks
4-5 cloves
½ teaspoon turmeric powder
A pinch of saffron
2 tablespoons skimmed milk
1 tablespoon rice bran oil
½ teaspoon caraway seeds
½ tablespoon ginger-garlic paste
2-3 green chillies, chopped
5 onions, sliced and sautéed till brown
1 teaspoon *garam masala* powder
1 tablespoon chopped fresh coriander
½ cup skimmed milk yogurt
A few sprigs fresh mint, torn
2 tablespoons lemon juice

Method

❶ Soak the rice for half an hour. Boil in three cups of water with salt and half of the green cardamoms, cinnamon and cloves till almost done. Drain.

❷ Soak the split Bengal gram for half an hour. Boil in one cup of water with salt and half of the turmeric powder till just cooked. Soak the saffron in milk and set aside.

❸ Heat the oil in a non-stick pan, add the remaining green cardamoms, cinnamon and cloves and sauté till fragrant.

❹ Add the caraway seeds and when they splutter, add the ginger-garlic paste and sauté.

❺ Add the green chillies and a little of the sautéed onions.

❻ Add the cooked Bengal gram, *garam masala* powder, fresh coriander and stir to mix well.

❼ Add the remaining turmeric powder, stir and remove from heat. Add the yogurt and mix well.

❽ Transfer half of the Bengal gram mixture into a separate pan.

❾ Spread half the rice over the Bengal gram mixture; sprinkle half of the remaining sautéed onions, fresh mint, lemon juice and saffron-flavoured milk.

❿ Spread the remaining Bengal gram over the rice followed by another layer of rice, sautéed onions, *garam masala* powder, fresh mint, lemon juice and saffron-flavoured milk.

⓫ Cover the pan tightly and cook on *dum* for twenty to twenty-five minutes and serve hot.

This delectable rice dish gets its name from the word *qabooli* which means acceptance. I would suggest this preparation for growing kids as they need protein-rich foods and Bengal gram is a good source.

tex mex pasta

Ingredients

200 grams fettuccine
1 teaspoon oil
1 tablespoon garlic-and-chilli
flavoured olive oil
½ medium zucchini, cut into strips
1 small red capsicum, seeded and cut
into strips
1 small yellow capsicum, seeded and
cut into strips
1 small green capsicum, seeded and
cut into strips
Salt to taste

To serve
8-10 tortilla chips
½ cup grated mozzarella cheese
2 jalapeño chillies, sliced

Salsa
1 tablespoon oil
4 garlic cloves, crushed
1 small onion, chopped
2 fresh red chillies, chopped
½ small green capsicum, chopped
½ teaspoon roasted cumin powder
1 teaspoon red chilli powder
1 cup tomato purée
Salt to taste
1 tablespoon lemon juice
2 tablespoons chopped fresh coriander

Method

❶ Preheat an oven to 180°C/350°F/Gas Mark 4.

❷ Bring sufficient water to boil and cook the pasta in it for five to seven minutes or till *al dente* (cooked but still firm to the bite), stirring gently all the while. Drain and refresh in cold water. Stir in the oil and set aside.

❸ For the salsa, heat the oil in a non-stick pan and sauté the garlic and onion. Add the red chillies, capsicum, roasted cumin powder, chilli powder and tomato purée. Stir well and add salt to taste. Cook for two to three minutes and remove from heat. When cooled, add the lemon juice and fresh coriander.

❹ In another pan, heat the garlic-and-chilli-flavoured olive oil and add the strips of zucchini and the red, yellow and green capsicums. Add salt to taste and stir-fry for three to four minutes. Add the boiled fettuccine and sauté. Add the salsa and mix well.

❺ Crumble the tortilla chips and line the bottom of a large baking dish. Spread the pasta over the layer of chips and cover with grated mozzarella cheese. Place the jalapeño chillies on top and bake in the preheated oven for six to seven minutes or till the cheese melts completely.

❻ Serve hot.

Fuse some Italian with Mexican and come up with a blockbuster! Today's youngsters enjoy international foods and fusion foods. This has high visual and nutritional appeal!

healthy protein pulao

Ingredients

1 cup soya granules, soaked in 1 cup water
1½ cups Basmati rice, soaked
2 tablespoons rice bran oil
½ teaspoon cumin seeds
1 inch cinnamon
3-4 cloves
2-3 green cardamoms
3 medium onions, chopped
1 inch ginger, chopped
10 garlic cloves, chopped
1½ tablespoons red chilli powder
¼ teaspoon turmeric powder
1 tablespoon coriander powder
3-4 large tomatoes, chopped
1 cup green peas, parboiled
Salt to taste
2 tablespoons chopped fresh coriander
3 cups Vegetable Stock (Vol. 5, page 66)

Method

❶ Heat the oil in a non-stick deep pan. Add the cumin seeds, cinnamon, cloves, green cardamoms and onions. Sauté for two minutes, add the ginger and garlic and sauté for another minute.

❷ Add the chilli, turmeric and coriander powders and continue to sauté. Add a little water to prevent the *masala* from scorching.

❸ Add the tomatoes and soya granules. Cook for a minute before adding the green peas, salt and fresh coriander.

❹ Add the rice and mix. Stir in the vegetable stock. Bring to a boil, lower the heat, cover and cook till the rice is done.

❺ Serve hot with any *raita*.

Soya granules are one of the richest sources of vegetable protein. The *pulao* is good for those who require large amounts of protein - teenagers, pregnant and lactating women.

cauliflower and lemon rice

Ingredients

500 grams cauliflower, separated into florets and blanched
2 tablespoons lemon juice
1 cup brown Basmati rice
Salt to taste
A pinch of sugar
4 green chillies, roughly chopped
3 dried red chillies, broken
2 tablespoons coriander seeds
5-6 cashew nuts, roughly chopped
¼ teaspoon turmeric powder
1 teaspoon olive oil
¼ teaspoon mustard seeds
½ teaspoon split skinless black gram
A pinch of fenugreek seeds
A pinch of asafoetida
7-8 curry leaves

Method

❶ Soak the rice in two cups water for two hours. Drain the rice, then boil in five cups of water until just cooked, ensuring that each grain is separate. Drain and set aside.

❷ Mix the salt and sugar with the lemon juice. Set aside.

❸ Grind the green and red chillies, coriander seeds, cashew nuts and turmeric powder to a fine paste, adding water as required.

❹ Heat the oil in a non-stick *kadai*. Add the mustard seeds, black gram and fenugreek seeds and sauté until the black gram turn light brown. Stir in the asafoetida and curry leaves and sauté for thirty seconds.

❺ Add the *masala* paste and cauliflower and mix well. Add the rice and lemon juice mixture and mix lightly. Cover and cook until everything is heated through.

I have gone a couple of steps beyond the traditional lemon rice (of South India) by adding cauliflower and a rich *masala*. Enjoy with *dal* for a fragrant meal.

handi biryani

Ingredients

1½ cups long-grained rice, soaked and drained

1 medium carrot, cut into ½-inch cubes

¼ medium cauliflower, separated into small florets

10-15 French beans, cut into ½-inch pieces

½ cup green peas

4 medium onions

A few saffron threads

A few drops *kewra* water

Salt to taste

2-3 green cardamoms

1 black cardamom

2-3 cloves

1 inch cinnamon

1 bay leaf

3 teaspoons oil

½ teaspoon caraway seeds

½ tablespoon ginger paste

½ tablespoon garlic paste

4-5 green chillies, chopped

1 tablespoon coriander powder

1 teaspoon turmeric powder

1 teaspoon red chilli powder

¾ cup skimmed milk yogurt

2 medium tomatoes, chopped

½ teaspoon *garam masala* powder

2 tablespoons chopped fresh coriander

2 tablespoons chopped fresh mint

1 tablespoon ghee

1 inch ginger, cut into thin strips

Method

❶ Chop one onion and slice the others. Soak the saffron in *kewra* water.

❷ Boil the rice in four cups of salted boiling water with the green cardamoms, black cardamom, cloves, cinnamon and bay leaf, until three-fourth done. Drain and set aside.

❸ Mix the carrot, cauliflower, French beans and peas and boil in three cups of salted water till three-fourth done. Drain and refresh under running water. Set aside.

❹ Heat half the oil in a non-stick pan and sauté the sliced onions till golden brown. Drain on absorbent paper and set aside.

❺ Heat the remaining oil in a thick-bottomed pan. Add the caraway seeds and when they begin to change colour, add the chopped onions and sauté until golden brown.

❻ Add the ginger paste, garlic paste and green chillies and stir. Add the coriander, turmeric and chilli powders and yogurt and mix well. Add the tomatoes and cook on medium heat till the oil separates from the *masala*. Add the boiled vegetables and salt and mix well.

❼ Arrange alternate layers of the cooked vegetables and rice in a *handi*. Sprinkle saffron-flavoured *kewra* water, *garam masala* powder, fresh coriander, fresh mint, sautéed onions and ghee over each layer and on top. Make sure that you end with the rice layer topped with the saffron and spices.

❽ Cover and seal with aluminum foil or *roti* dough. Keep the *handi* on a *tawa* and cook on low heat for twenty minutes.

❾ Serve hot with a *raita* of your choice.

Use flamboyance when you serve *handi biryani*... open the seal slowly, so that the aroma wafting from it gives an indication of its wonderful contents! Since the vegetables have been cooked in a well-sealed container, they will be nutrient-dense.

clay pot rice

Ingredients

1 cup long-grained rice
600 grams boneless chicken, cut into ½-inch cubes
1 sausage, sliced
2½ cups Chicken Stock (Vol. 5, page 66)
Salt to taste
5 dried black mushrooms, soaked and quartered
1 inch ginger, sliced
1 spring onion, sliced

Marinade
1½ tablespoons olive oil
2 tablespoons oyster sauce
2 teaspoons soy sauce
2 teaspoons rice wine
½ teaspoon sesame oil
¾ teaspoon black soy sauce
1 teaspoon sugar
½ teaspoon white pepper powder

Method

❶ Place the rice with the stock and salt in a clay pot, cover and cook over low heat for about twenty minutes.

❷ Combine the marinade ingredients in a bowl, add the chicken and mix.

❸ Place the marinated chicken, sausage slices, mushrooms and ginger on top of the cooked rice. Cover and cook for another ten minutes.

❹ Sprinkle the spring onions and serve hot.

Simple to make and a convenient one-dish meal, everyone clamours for the crispy rice at the bottom of the pot!

erra saadam

Ingredients

2 cups cooled cooked brown Basmati rice
1 egg, beaten
450 grams small prawns, peeled and deveined
2 tablespoons rice bran oil
½ teaspoon mustard seeds
1 clove
1 green cardamom
½ inch cinnamon
1 bay leaf
2 large onions, chopped
2 garlic cloves, chopped
2 medium tomatoes,
cut into small pieces
½ teaspoon red chilli powder
Salt to taste
½ teaspoon turmeric powder
4-5 black peppercorns, crushed
1 tablespoon fennel seeds, powdered
2 tablespoons chopped fresh coriander

Method

❶ Heat the oil in a non-stick pan. Add the mustard seeds, clove, cardamom, cinnamon and bay leaf and sauté for a minute. Add the onions and garlic and sauté for about five minutes or until the onions are lightly browned.

❷ Lower the heat and add the tomatoes pressing them with the back of the spoon till all the moisture evaporates and the oil separates. Add the chilli powder, salt, turmeric powder and one-fourth of the crushed black peppercorns.

❸ Cook for a minute. Add the prawns and cook for five minutes, stirring occasionally.

❹ Stir in the powdered fennel, the remaining crushed peppercorns and a pinch of salt into the beaten egg and pour over the prawns. The egg should coat the prawns.

❺ Cook for another minute, add the rice and cook for two to three minutes or until the egg is cooked and the prawns are pink.

❻ Garnish with the fresh coriander and serve.

A healthy version of prawn *pulao* what with fibre-rich brown rice! Fibre is basically a very important nutrient as it gives a sense of fullness and improves the bowel movement. Prawns with eggs are good sources of protein.

seafood pad thai

Ingredients

12 small prawns, peeled and deveined
100 grams fish fillets,
cut into 1-inch pieces
8-10 mussels or clams
200 grams flat noodles, boiled
1½ tablespoons oil
5-6 spring onions, chopped
5-6 garlic cloves, chopped
1 medium green capsicum,
seeded and cut into thin strips
Salt to taste
1 teaspoon soy sauce
2 tablespoons brown sugar
2 fresh red chillies, diagonally sliced
5-6 stalks spring onion greens, chopped
2 tablespoons roasted peanuts,
coarsely ground
1 tablespoon lemon juice
½ cup bean sprouts

Method

❶ Pat dry the prawns with an absorbent kitchen towel. Prise open the mussels or clam shells with a knife and scoop out the meat.

❷ Heat the oil in a non-stick pan. Add the onions, garlic, prawns, fish and mussels or clams and capsicum and toss.

❸ Add the noodles, salt, soy sauce, brown sugar and toss some more.

❹ Add the red chillies and toss again. Add the spring onion greens and most of the roasted peanuts and toss.

❺ Transfer to a serving dish. Add the lemon juice and bean sprouts. Top with the remaining roasted peanuts and serve hot.

Chef's Note: Boil seven to eight cups of water in a large pan. Add the flat noodles and cook till *al dente* (just done). Drain and refresh in cold water. Spread it on a plate to cool.

Pad Thai or stir-fry is a popular Thai street food. This is a little more elaborate with prawns and other seafood added to it. Seafood has a good amount of selenium which is an antioxidant.

methods of cooking

Cooking enhances the taste of raw food, but it can also destroy the nutrients present in the food. How can the nutrient value of any food item be maintained or enhanced during cooking?

Food can be cooked using various methods like steaming, boiling, roasting, frying, stir-frying, sautéing, grilling, baking and microwaving. Ingredients can also be prepared before cooking by sprouting, parboiling, fermentation and parching.

Different foods require different methods of cooking. One can bake a cake but fry a pancake. One can also bake a cake in a microwave oven. No one would like steamed samosas, because they taste best fried, but you could bake them. And yes, we love steamed dimsums rather than fried ones. Vegetables are versatile because they can be steamed, boiled, fried, stir-fried, sautéed, grilled, baked and pressure-cooked.

steaming

Steaming is one of the best ways to cook food especially when you want to skimp on your calorie intake. Steamed foods retain nutrients, flavour, colour and texture and can be prepared without butter, oil or salt. Steamed foods are naturally moist and tender. In fact, all foods can be steamed successfully. Steamed foods are definitely lower in calories and fat than the same food either stir-fried or grilled. Hence, steamed foods are a boon for those on a restricted diet. In India *idlis* and *dhoklas* are very popular steamed snacks, so much so that there are special cookers available for these.

baking

Baking means cooking in dry heat in the oven, for example cakes, biscuits, casseroles, meat and vegetable preparations. The temperature of the oven can be altered, depending on the dish, usually between 150°C and 250°C.

barbecuing/tandoori

There is nothing more delicious than the smell of food cooking on the barbecue. Though this requires special equipment and space, it is worth it simply because meats, vegetables and fruits cooked in different marinades enhance the flavour. In India, tandoori cooking is similar to barbecuing. Tandoori cooking also requires one to marinate the raw food in a mixture of herbs, spices and yogurt that give it a distinctive red colour.

blanching

Fruit and vegetables are often blanched when they are fresh. This involves putting them very quickly in boiling water and then in iced water to stop the cooking process. The food can then be frozen, thus preserving the vitamins and colour. Vegetables such as spinach or cabbage are often blanched, as this takes away the bitter taste which can sometimes be found in these foods. Tomatoes, peaches and almonds are much easier to peel when they have been blanched.

frying

Not the healthiest way of cooking food, frying is the only way to prepare crisp chips, fish coated in batter, or vegetables. Frying is also a quicker way of cooking. The oil must be heated to a high temperature and then the food added. Shallow-frying is used for fish dipped in breadcrumbs, fried egg, pancakes and *dosas*. Deep-frying is the best way of cooking chips and batter-coated food. The food should be blotted on absorbent paper before being served, thus taking away a little, but not all of the unhealthy oil. Fried food should be crisp on the outside and soft on the inside. This is achieved by heating the oil to the right temperature - too hot and the food will burn, too low and the food will be soggy. Margarine or butter is not suitable for frying.

grilling

Grilling is the healthier alternative to frying foods. The food can be seasoned or basted with a little butter before it is grilled. This method is not as much used as it should be.

pressure-cooking

In this form of cooking, food is cooked in a third of the time it takes with conventional methods like boiling. The food is cooked under a very high pressure. The steam is trapped inside the cooker and since it is at a higher temperature than boiling water, the food is cooked more quickly. The nutrients are retained in the food and not leached out in the water which happens in boiling.

roasting

Meat and vegetables are cooked by roasting them dry or in a minimum amount of oil, in an oven, on an open fire or in a thick-bottomed pan. It differs from frying, because only a little oil or fat is used and the food is then left in the oven to cook, either quickly at a high temperature (over 200°C) or slowly. Roasting gives the food a crisp outer coating.

microwave-cooking

Microwave ovens use microwave radiation to penetrate the food. The radiation agitates water molecules in the food, creating friction and heat. This energy then spreads throughout the food by conduction and by convection in liquids. It is a faster method of cooking but has its downside. The food does not brown or become crisp like it does in normal sautéing or roasting.

stir-frying

Made popular by the Chinese, stir-frying is a method of frying uniformly-sized pieces of food, quickly, with a small amount of fat over very high heat. Vegetables remain crunchy with their natural juices sealed in.

dalskadhis

vrat ki kadhi

Ingredients

1¾ cups skimmed milk yogurt
2 tablespoons water chestnut flour
¼ teaspoon rock salt
1 teaspoon red chilli powder
¼ teaspoon cinnamon powder
2 tablespoons pure ghee
1 teaspoon cumin seeds
3-4 dried red chillies, broken
10-12 curry leaves
½ teaspoon sugar
Salt to taste
1 tablespoon chopped fresh coriander

Method

❶ Add the water chestnut flour, rock salt, chilli powder and cinnamon powder to the yogurt and whisk well. Add four cups of water and mix well.

❷ Heat the ghee in a *kadai*. Add the cumin seeds, chillies and curry leaves. Sauté till the cumin seeds splutter. Add the yogurt mixture and cook till the *kadhi* thickens slightly. Stir in the sugar and salt. Cook over low heat for two minutes.

❸ Garnish with the fresh coriander and serve hot.

The use of water chestnut flour makes this a valid addition to fasting recipes. I like to make this *kadhi* even otherwise as it is much lighter than the one made using gram flour.

aamras ki kadhi

Ingredients

1 cup unripe green mango pulp
1 cup ripe mango pulp
3 tablespoons gram flour
Salt to taste
1 cup buttermilk
2 teaspoons oil
A pinch of asafoetida
½ teaspoon mustard seeds
¼ teaspoon fenugreek seeds
6-8 curry leaves
2 green chillies, slit
¼ cup *boondi*

Method

❶ Mix together the unripe green mango pulp, ripe mango pulp, gram flour and salt to a smooth mixture. Add the buttermilk and mix again.

❷ Heat the oil in a deep pan. Add the asafoetida, mustard seeds, fenugreek seeds and sauté. Add the curry leaves and green chillies and sauté for two minutes. Add the mango mixture and mix. Add a little water if required and bring to a boil. Lower the heat and simmer for ten to fifteen minutes. Adjust the consistency by adding two cups of water.

❸ Add the *boondi* and simmer for five more minutes. Serve hot.

Must-have in the mango season! If you want to skip the unripe green mango increase the amount of buttermilk but ensure that it is sour. Mangoes are a storehouse of Vitamin A and unripe green mangoes help to beat the heat.

methiwali arhar dal

Ingredients

1 cup split pigeon peas
½ teaspoon turmeric powder
Salt to taste
½ teaspoon red chilli powder
1 teaspoon grated jaggery

Seasoning
½ medium bunch (150 grams) fresh fenugreek,
chopped
1 tablespoon pure ghee
¼ teaspoon asafoetida
6 garlic cloves, peeled

Method

❶ Soak the pigeon peas in two cups of water for one
hour. Drain.

❷ Pressure cook the pigeon peas in three cups of
water with the turmeric powder in a pressure cooker
till pressure is released four times (four whistles).
Remove the lid when the pressure reduces and mash
the *dal* well.

❸ Add half a cup of water, salt, chilli powder and
jaggery. Bring to a boil.

❹ For the seasoning, heat the ghee in a pan and add
the asafoetida and garlic cloves.

❺ Sauté till the garlic turns a light brown.

❻ Add the fresh fenugreek and sauté for one to two
minutes. Pour the seasoning on the *dal* and stir well.

❼ Adjust the consistency if needed. Serve hot.

Trust the greens to add flavour and nutrition to
any daily *dal*! Fresh fenugreek adds iron, calcium
and Vitamin A and the jaggery adds a full-bodied
sweetness to its slight bitterness.

khatti meethi dal

Ingredients

1 cup split pigeon peas
¼ teaspoon asafoetida
½ teaspoon crushed fenugreek seeds
1 medium tomato, chopped
½ teaspoon green chilli-ginger paste
7-8 curry leaves
½ teaspoon turmeric powder
½ teaspoon red chilli powder
¼ teaspoon coriander powder
¼ teaspoon cumin powder
Salt to taste
3-4 *kokum* rinds
2 tablespoons grated jaggery
1 tablespoon raw peanuts
1 tablespoon chopped fresh coriander

Seasoning
1 tablespoon oil
1 round dried red round chilli
½ teaspoon mustard seeds
½ teaspoon cumin seeds
A pinch of asafoetida

Method

❶ Soak the split pigeon peas in two cups of water for one hour. Drain and pressure-cook in three cups of water with asafoetida and fenugreek seeds in a pressure cooker till the pressure is released four times (four whistles). Remove the lid when the pressure reduces completely.

❷ Transfer into a thick-bottomed pan. Add one-and-a-half cups of water and the tomato. Process with a hand blender till smooth.

❸ Place on heat and add the green chilli-ginger paste, curry leaves, turmeric, chilli, coriander and cumin powders, salt, *kokum*, jaggery and peanuts one by one, stirring continuously.

❹ Bring to a boil, lower the heat and simmer for twelve to fifteen minutes. Adjust the consistency by adding water. Remove from heat. Sprinkle the fresh coriander.

❺ For the seasoning, heat the oil in a small pan. Add the red chilli, mustard seeds and cumin seeds. As the mustard seeds begin to splutter, add the asafoetida and immediately pour over the fresh coriander. This ensures that the fresh coriander remains green. Cover the pan with a lid immediately to trap the flavours.

❻ Place the pan on heat again and bring to a boil. Adjust the consistency and salt.

❼ Serve hot with rice.

Chef's Tip: You can add chopped dried dates for added texture and taste.

Pigeon peas or *toovar dal* is a daily *dal* in most homes in western and southern India. And the Gujarati way of making it sweet and sour is unique what with *methi dana*, *gur* and *kokum*. I enjoy the peanuts as they add a crunchy texture.

banjari dal

Ingredients

⅔ cup split black gram with skin, soaked

⅓ cup split Bengal gram, soaked

¼ teaspoon turmeric powder

Salt to taste

1½ tablespoons pure ghee

2 small onions, sliced

2 cloves

1-inch cinnamon stick

3 dried red chillies, broken

1½ teaspoons ginger-garlic paste

1½ teaspoons coriander powder

2 green chillies, chopped

¼ teaspoon black pepper powder

¾ teaspoon red chilli powder

1 tablespoon chopped fresh coriander

1 inch ginger, cut into thin strips

Method

❶ Pressure-cook together both kinds of split gram, the turmeric powder, salt and three cups of water till the pressure is released four to five times (four to five whistles) or until done.

❷ Heat the ghee in a pan, add the onions, cloves, cinnamon and dried red chillies and sauté till the onions turn golden.

❸ Add the ginger-garlic paste, coriander powder, green chillies, pepper powder and chilli powder and sauté for a couple of minutes.

❹ Add to the cooked gram and boil for five minutes. Transfer to a serving bowl.

❺ Garnish with the fresh coriander and ginger strips and serve hot.

This thick *dal* is wonderful with *roti* and will transport you to the time of the Rajputana royals coming back to camp after a good hunt. *Dals* are an excellent source of protein.

gujarati kadhi

Ingredients

2½ cups skimmed milk yogurt
1½ tablespoons gram flour
1 tablespoon grated jaggery
2 green chillies, minced
Salt to taste
1 teaspoon olive oil
½ teaspoon mustard seeds
½ teaspoon cumin seeds
8-10 curry leaves
2 dried red chillies, broken in half
3-4 cloves
½ inch cinnamon stick
A pinch of asafoetida

Method

❶ Whisk together the gram flour and yogurt in a deep pan until smooth. Add four cups of water, mix well, Add the jaggery and green chillies.

❷ Cook on a low heat, stirring continuously, till the *kadhi* attains a moderately thick consistency. Add the salt to taste.

❸ Heat the oil in a small pan, add the mustard and cumin seeds, curry leaves, red chillies, cloves, cinnamon and asafoetida. When the mustard seeds begin to splutter, pour the sizzling spices into the *kadhi* and mix well.

❹ Serve hot with rice.

For some time after I got married to Alyona, I used to enjoy this *kadhi* as a soup! Now I have learnt to eat it the traditional way, served piping hot and mixed with steamed rice. You can make the meal healthier by having steamed brown rice instead of white rice.

punjabi kadhi

Ingredients

1 cup yogurt
¼ cup gram flour
1 teaspoon turmeric powder
Salt to taste
1 tablespoon olive oil
½ teaspoon fenugreek seeds
½ teaspoon cumin seeds
6 black peppercorns
2 dried red chillies, broken
1 medium onion, sliced
½ inch ginger, chopped
1 teaspoon red chilli powder
2 tablespoons chopped fresh coriander

Method

❶ Whisk the yogurt and gram flour together till smooth. Add the turmeric powder, salt and three cups of water.

❷ Heat the oil in a non-stick *kadai*. Add the fenugreek seeds, cumin seeds, peppercorns and red chillies. Stir-fry for half a minute. Add the onion and ginger and stir-fry for a minute. Add the yogurt mixture. Bring to a boil, lower the heat and simmer for about fifteen minutes, stirring occasionally.

❸ Add the chilli powder and continue to simmer for four to five minutes.

❹ Garnish with the fresh coriander and serve hot with steamed rice.

My most favourite comfort food. I love coming home to *kadhi chawal* after a trip abroad… because I miss it so. *Kadhi* is an excellent way of including yogurt in the menu. It can be eaten by dieters too as a change from *dal*. Fenugreek seeds are rich in Vitamin A, calcium, iron and fibre.

punjabi rajma

Ingredients

1½ cups red kidney beans,
soaked overnight
1½ tablespoons rice bran oil
2 bay leaves
2 medium onions, chopped
1 inch ginger, chopped
6-8 garlic cloves, chopped
2 teaspoons red chilli powder
1 tablespoon coriander powder
½ teaspoon turmeric powder
1 teaspoon cumin powder
3 medium tomatoes, chopped
Salt to taste
1 teaspoon *garam masala* powder
1 tablespoon chopped fresh coriander

Method

❶ Pressure-cook the beans with five cups of water in a pressure cooker till the pressure is released five times (five whistles) or till completely cooked.

❷ Heat the oil in a deep non-stick pan. Add the bay leaves and onions and sauté till golden.

❸ Add the ginger and garlic and continue to sauté for a minute.

❹ Add the chilli, coriander, turmeric and cumin powders and stir. Add the tomatoes and salt and cook till the tomatoes are done and the oil separates from the *masala*.

❺ Add the cooked beans along with the cooking liquid and mix. Cook on low heat for fifteen minutes stirring in between. Adjust the salt and add the *garam masala* powder. Cook for five minutes.

❻ Garnish with the fresh coriander and serve hot with steamed rice.

This is one preparation that reminds me of my childhood Saturday afternoons... *rajma* in its gravy, garnished with fresh coriander, hot fluffy Basmati rice and thinly sliced onions doused in lemon juice. No wonder it is still my favourite meal!

sambhar

Ingredients

½ cup split pigeon peas, soaked
¼ teaspoon turmeric powder
4 teaspoons rice bran oil
1 lemon-sized ball of tamarind
½ teaspoon mustard seeds
4 dried red chillies, halved
½ teaspoon fenugreek seeds, optional
¼ teaspoon asafoetida
4 green chillies, slit
10-12 curry leaves
2 drumsticks, cut into 2½-inch pieces
1½ teaspoons *sambhar* powder
Salt to taste
1 teaspoon rice flour
¼ cup chopped fresh coriander

Method

❶ Pressure-cook the pigeon peas in two-and-a-half cups of water with the turmeric powder and one teaspoon oil in a pressure cooker till the pressure is released three times (three whistles). Remove the lid once the pressure has reduced completely. Mash the cooked *dal* lightly with back of a ladle

❷ Soak the tamarind in one cup of warm water, remove the pulp, strain and set aside.

❸ Heat the remaining oil in a thick-bottomed pan. Add the mustard seeds. When they splutter add the red chillies, fenugreek seeds and asafoetida.

❹ Stir and add the green chillies, curry leaves and drumsticks and cook for one minute on medium heat stirring briefly.

❺ Add the tamarind pulp, *sambhar* powder, salt and one cup water.

❻ Reduce the heat and simmer for six to eight minutes or till the drumsticks are cooked. Add the boiled *dal* and simmer for two to three minutes.

❼ Blend the rice flour in a quarter cup water and add to the *sambhar*. Stir well and cook further for two to three minutes, stirring occasionally.

❽ Sprinkle the fresh coriander and serve hot.

Chef's Tip: You can use different vegetables like white radish, ladies' fingers, pumpkin, brinjal, *sambhar* onions, etc., either individually or in any combination.

This is a typical South Indian dish with balanced nutrients. There would probably be as many recipes of *sambhar* as there are households in South India! Every family has its own recipe, its own secret *masala*... you can try out what I have given here and then start work on customizing your recipe! Drumsticks are a good source of Vitamin A, C and minerals like calcium.

sindhi kadhi

Ingredients

½ cup split pigeon peas
3 medium tomatoes
3 teaspoons rice bran oil
¾ teaspoon cumin seeds
¼ teaspoon fenugreek seeds
A pinch of asafoetida (optional)
3 tablespoons gram flour
6-8 small ladies' fingers, slit
2-3 green chillies, slit
10-12 cluster beans
Salt to taste
1 teaspoon red chilli powder
¼ teaspoon turmeric powder
2 tablespoons tamarind pulp
7-8 curry leaves

Method

❶ Soak the pigeon peas in two cups of water for about half an hour. Drain.

❷ Pressure-cook the pigeon peas along with the halved tomatoes and two cups of water in a pressure cooker till the pressure is released three times (three whistles) or till done.

❸ Remove the lid when the pressure has reduced completely. Mash the *dal* well and pass through a strainer pressing the *dal* through with the back of a ladle. Heat one teaspoon oil in a non-stick deep pan. Add half a teaspoon of cumin seeds and fenugreek seeds. Add the asafoetida.

❹ When the cumin seeds begin to change colour, add the gram flour and roast for about five minutes. Add three cups of water, a little at a time, stirring continuously to prevent lumps from forming. Heat one teaspoon oil in another pan. Add the ladies' fingers and sauté for one or two minutes.

❺ Add the green chillies and cluster beans and continue to sauté for two or three minutes.

❻ Add the mashed *dal*, salt, chilli powder and turmeric powder and mix. Add a little water to the tamarind pulp and stir it into the *kadhi*. Add the sautéed vegetables and mix.

❼ In another pan, heat the remaining oil and add the remaining cumin seeds and curry leaves. When the cumin seeds change colour, add it to the *kadhi*.

❽ Serve hot with steamed rice.

Full of vegetables that complement each other in taste, texture and colour, this *kadhi* is a visual delight. I recommend that you make only as much as will be consumed because it will not keep well in the refrigerator.

dal chenchki

Ingredients

1 cup split red lentils
1 tablespoon rice bran oil
8-10 baby onions, peeled
½ teaspoon cumin seeds
¼ teaspoon *panch phoron*
1 medium tomato, chopped
1 teaspoon red chilli powder
½ teaspoon turmeric powder
Salt to taste
½ teaspoon sugar
2 tablespoons chopped fresh coriander

Method

❶ Soak the lentils in three cups of water for fifteen minutes. Drain, spread on a large *thali* or plate and leave it to dry.

❷ Heat the oil in a non-stick *kadai*. Add the baby onions and fry lightly till brown.

❸ Add the cumin seeds, *panch phoron*, tomato, chilli powder, turmeric powder and salt and sauté for two minutes.

❹ Add the lentils and sugar with one cup of water. Cover and continue cooking on medium heat.

❺ Take care that the lentils are not mashed and the grains remain separate. It should be dry with practically no gravy. Serve hot garnished with the fresh coriander.

Note: Panch Phoron is a mixture of equal quantities of cumin seeds, mustard seeds, fennel seeds, fenugreek seeds and onion seeds.

Panch phoron is the famous spice used in Bengali cuisine. This *dal* requires a little practice to make as the first few attempts can give a mushy finish... blame it on the red lentils as it does cook fast! All in all, a nutritious protein-packed accompaniment.

tomato rasam

Ingredients

2 medium tomatoes, chopped
4 tablespoons split pigeon peas
½ lemon-sized ball of tamarind
¼ cup chopped fresh coriander
2 dried red chillies, broken
1½ teaspoons *rasam* powder
¼ teaspoon asafoetida
Salt to taste
10-12 curry leaves
2 tablespoons pure ghee
½ teaspoon mustard seeds

Method

❶ Wash, drain and cook the split pigeon peas in two cups of water until soft. Strain and mash them well. Reserve the strained cooking liquid.

❷ Soak the tamarind in one cup of warm water; squeeze out the pulp, strain and reserve.

❸ Reserve two tablespoons of the chopped fresh coriander to garnish. Mix the tamarind pulp with the remaining fresh coriander, *rasam* powder, asafoetida, salt and half the quantity of curry leaves in a deep pan. Bring to a boil, lower heat and simmer for two or three minutes.

❹ Add the tomatoes and the reserved cooking liquid. Simmer for four to five minutes and add the mashed *dal*. Stir well and cook for another minute.

❺ Remove from the heat and sprinkle the reserved fresh coriander.

❻ Heat the pure ghee in a pan, add the mustard seeds and when they splutter add the chillies and remaining curry leaves and stir well. Pour the sizzling spices over the *rasam* and cover immediately to trap the flavours. Serve hot.

Chef's Tip: Traditionally all *rasams* are boiled in a vessel made from a special alloy. This gives a unique flavour to the preparation.

Call it *rasam, chaaru* or *saaru* in any South Indian language the recipe will have the imprint of the cook! This recipe relies heavily on tomatoes for the essential sourness. *Rasam* can be served with rice or you can strain this *rasam* and serve it in small tumblers with a lemon wedge, as an appetizer.

leeli tuvar ni kadhi

Ingredients

½ cup fresh green pigeon peas, boiled and drained
4 tablespoons gram flour
2 cups skimmed milk yogurt
2 tablespoons pure ghee
1 teaspoon carom seeds
4 dried red button chillies
1 inch ginger, chopped
2 teaspoons garlic paste
3 green chillies, chopped
8-10 curry leaves
A pinch of asafoetida
2 medium brinjals, diced
Salt to taste
2 teaspoons sugar
1 tablespoon chopped fresh coriander

Method

❶ Whisk the gram flour and yogurt together. Add four cups of water and whisk till smooth.

❷ Heat the ghee in a deep pan. Add the carom seeds, button chillies, ginger, garlic paste, green chillies and curry leaves and sauté for two minutes. Add the asafoetida and brinjals and sauté for two minutes.

❸ Add the boiled fresh green pigeon peas and sauté for a minute. Add the yogurt mixture. Bring to a boil. Add the salt and sugar and simmer, stirring gently, for ten to fifteen minutes or till thickened to the desired consistency.

❹ Garnish with the fresh coriander and serve hot.

Fresh, tender pigeon peas are available only in the winter months. Enterprising Gujaratis store them in the freezer for use all year round. Fresh green pigeon peas are a good source of protein. Carom seeds reduce the acidic effect of the pigeon peas.

dal lucknowi

Ingredients

1 cup split pigeon peas, soaked
2 green chillies, chopped
½ teaspoon turmeric powder
Salt to taste
1 tablespoon rice bran oil
1 teaspoon cumin seeds
4 dried red chillies, broken
5 garlic cloves, chopped
A pinch of asafoetida
1 cup skimmed milk
2 tablespoons chopped fresh coriander

Method

❶ Pressure-cook the split pigeon peas and green chillies with two cups of water in a pressure cooker till the pressure is released twice (two whistles). Remove the lid when the pressure has reduced completely. Add the turmeric powder and salt and simmer on low heat.

❷ Heat the oil in a non-stick pan. Add the cumin seeds, red chillies, garlic and asafoetida and sauté till fragrant. Pour the sizzling spices into the simmering *dal* and mix well. Add one cup of water and milk and continue to simmer for two to three minutes.

❸ Adjust the salt, garnish with the fresh coriander and serve hot.

This *dal* has a smoother and fuller texture as there is milk in it... an ingredient which will surprise many. Skimmed milk adds to the protein and calcium content.

ickles chutneys

gor keri

Ingredients

1 kilogram unripe mangoes, peeled and
cut into ½-inch cubes
6 teaspoons salt
1 teaspoon turmeric powder ·
1 kilogram grated jaggery
200 grams pickle *masala*
1 tablespoon fennel seeds

Pickle *masala*
100 grams split mustard seeds, lightly roasted
100 grams split fenugreek seeds, lightly roasted
100 grams split coriander seeds, lightly roasted
300 grams red chilli powder
½ teaspoon turmeric powder
1 teaspoon asafoetida
¼ cup oil, smoked and cooled

Method

❶ Combine the split mustard, fenugreek and
coriander seeds, chilli powder, turmeric powder
and asafoetida in a deep bowl and mix. Add
the oil and mix again. You can store this in an
airtight jar to be used when required.

❷ Add the salt and one teaspoon turmeric
powder to the mango cubes in a large glass
bowl and mix well. Cover and set aside for five to
six hours. During this time, the mango cubes will
release water.

❸ Drain the mango cubes and spread
them on a large plate and dry in the sun
for about six hours.

❹ Place the dried mango cubes in a large
glass bowl. Add the jaggery, pickle *masala*
and fennel seeds and mix well. Cover and
set aside for six to eight days stirring twice
daily till all the jaggery has melted.

❺ Store in sterilized airtight glass or
porcelain jars.

Gor keri, in literal translation, means
jaggery mango... that is true of this typical
Gujarati pickle as the unripe mango is
soaked in loads of jaggery! Unripe mangoes
are great in reducing acidity, improving
digestion and giving a cooling effect.

teekha nimbu achaar

Ingredients

6 large lemons, quartered and seeded
¼ cup salt
½ cup sugar
2 inches ginger, crushed
8 green chillies, chopped
2-3 tablespoons red chilli powder
1 tablespoon roasted mustard seeds
1 teaspoon roasted fenugreek seeds
2 star anise, roasted

Method

❶ Place the lemons in a large bowl and sprinkle salt over them. Cover and leave aside for one day. On the following day, toss the lemons in the juice that has formed.

❷ Take four quarters of the salted lemons and squeeze out the juice in a small pan. Add the sugar, ginger and three tablespoons water. Bring to a boil, and cook on low heat, stirring continuously, till the sugar dissolves completely.

❸ Add the green chillies and red chilli powder. Cook for one minute. Set aside and allow to cool.

❹ Add the roasted mustard seeds, roasted fenugreek seeds and roasted star anise. Mix well.

❺ Pour the remaining lemon quarters into a sterilized glass jar. Pour over the sugar-chilli mix, covering them completely. Press the lemons down so that they are soaked completely. Cover the jar with a lid and set aside for twenty-five to twenty-eight days for the pickle to mature.

Top a hot *lachcha parantha* with a dollop of butter and a bit of this *achaar* and... need I say more? Pickles are needed to make the daily meal more satisfying to the taste buds. This one is prepared with many healthy ingredients like ginger, mustard seeds, fenugreek seeds and lemons.

tamatar ki chutney

Ingredients

7-8 medium tomatoes, finely chopped
1 tablespoon pure ghee
½ teaspoon cumin seeds
A pinch of asafoetida
1 green chilli, broken
10 curry leaves
½ teaspoon red chilli powder
¼ teaspoon turmeric powder
1 teaspoon coriander powder
½ teaspoon cumin powder
½ teaspoon *garam masala* powder
Salt to taste
1 teaspoon sugar
2 tablespoons chopped fresh coriander

Method

❶ Heat the ghee in a pan. Add the cumin seeds and when they begin to change colour, add the asafoetida, green chilli and curry leaves and sauté for a minute.

❷ Mix together the chilli powder, turmeric powder, coriander powder, cumin powder and *garam masala* powder in one-fourth cup of water and add to the green chilli mixture. Sauté for two minutes.

❸ Add the tomatoes, salt, sugar and half a cup of water. Mix well. Lower the heat once the mixture comes to a boil and cook for ten to fifteen minutes.

❹ Garnish with the fresh coriander and serve hot.

Let's replace the ubiquitous tomato ketchup or tomato sauce with a healthier option like this *Tamatar ki Chutney*. Tomatoes are a rich source of Vitamin C, which helps in building up immunity. Curry leaves, with their essential oils, add flavour, fibre and help in digestion.

red chilli-garlic chutney

Ingredients

10 dried red chillies, seeded
12 large garlic cloves
1½ tablespoons lemon juice
Sea salt to taste
1 teaspoon cumin powder

Method

❶ Soak the red chillies in one-and-a-half cups of water for half an hour. Drain.

❷ Grind the red chillies and garlic cloves with lemon juice to a fine paste. Add a little water if necessary.

❸ Add the sea salt and cumin powder and mix well.

❹ Use as a topping on *bhelpuri* or any *chaat*.

This chutney is a great saviour for those who prefer the food a little spicy... it keeps well bottled, too. Eating raw garlic does not come easy for all, so such chutneys are ideal. Garlic, belonging to the same *Allium* family as onions and leeks, controls cholesterol, protects against skin infections and lowers blood pressure. It also aids digestion.

sarson ki chutney

Ingredients

½ cup mustard seeds
1½ cups + 4 tablespoons vinegar
Salt to taste
1 tablespoon sugar
¼ teaspoon turmeric powder

Method

❶ Grind the mustard seeds with four tablespoons of vinegar to a fine paste.

❷ Place the remaining vinegar in a pan. Add the salt, sugar and turmeric powder and bring to a boil.

❸ Add the mustard paste and cook for fifteen to twenty minutes or till thick.

❹ Cool and serve.

Chef's Tip: For best results mature for two days and then serve.

Our very own *desi* mustard paste... companion to many *kababs*. Mustard seeds are a good source of omega-3 fatty acids and low in fat and sodium. They also contain magnesium and potassium.

kairi ki launjee

Ingredients

1 kilogram unripe mangoes
3 tablespoons mustard oil
¾ teaspoon fenugreek seeds
4 teaspoons fennel seeds
½ teaspoon onion seeds
1 teaspoon coriander powder
1 teaspoon red chilli powder
½ teaspoon turmeric powder
Salt to taste
1¼ cups grated jaggery

Method

❶ Peel the mangoes, cut lengthways into quarters and remove the kernels.

❷ Heat the oil in a *kadai* to smoking point. Lower to medium heat, add the fenugreek seeds and sauté till they begin to change colour.

❸ Add the fennel seeds, onion seeds, coriander powder, chilli powder, turmeric powder and salt and stir.

❹ Add the mangoes and stir for five minutes.

❺ Add the jaggery and half a cup of water. Bring to a boil, cover and simmer, stirring occasionally, for seven to eight minutes.

❻ Remove from heat and cool. Store in sterilized bottles.

Fenugreek seeds, used for the seasoning of *kairi ki launjee*, are known to lower the blood cholesterol levels. Mustard oil is also low in fat and sodium. Unripe mangoes should be eaten when in season for overall health.

green chutney

Ingredients

1 cup fresh coriander, chopped
½ cup fresh mint, chopped
2-3 green chillies, chopped
Black salt to taste
¼ teaspoon sugar
1 teaspoon lemon juice

Method

❶ Process the fresh coriander and mint with the green chillies in a blender.

❷ Make a smooth paste using a little water if required. Add the salt and sugar.

❸ Transfer to a bowl and stir in the lemon juice and mix well.

Chef's Tip: To add sourness you can use crushed dried pomegranate seeds or dried mango powder instead of lemon juice. In season unripe green mango is a good substitute.

Variation: Add yogurt to the chutney and mix properly (one cup yogurt for two tablespoons of chutney).

Coriander is a herb that has been in use in ancient Indian cookery. It is soothing to the stomach and its long-term use strengthens the stomach muscles. Coriander is - like any other green leafy vegetable - high in fibre and is beneficial for diabetics and heart patients.